Pioneer Life
in the
American West

Christy Steele

WORLD ALMANAC® LIBRARY

Please visit our web site at: www.worldalmanaclibrary.com
For a free color catalog describing World Almanac® Library's list of high-quality books
and multimedia programs, call 1-800-848-2928 (USA) or 1-800-387-3178 (Canada).
World Almanac® Library's fax: (414) 332-3567.

Library of Congress Cataloging-in-Publication Data

Steele, Christy, 1970-
   Pioneer life in the American West / by Christy Steele.
      p. cm. — (America's westward expansion)
   Includes bibliographical references and index.
   ISBN 0-8368-5790-9 (lib. bdg.)
   ISBN 0-8368-5797-6 (softcover)
   1. Frontier and pioneer life—West (U.S.)—Juvenile literature.   2. Pioneers—
West (U.S.)—History—Juvenile literature.   3. West (U.S.)—History—19th
century—Juvenile literature.   4. West (U.S.)—History—1890-1945—Juvenile
literature.   5. United States—Territorial expansion—Juvenile literature.   I. Title.
F596.S8265   2005
978'.01—dc22   2004056772

First published in 2005 by
World Almanac® Library
330 West Olive Street, Suite 100
Milwaukee, WI 53212 USA

Copyright © 2005 by World Almanac® Library.

Produced by: EMC—The Education Matters Company
Editors: Christy Steele, Rachael Taaffe
Designer and page production: Jennifer Pfeiffer
Maps and diagrams: Jennifer Pfeiffer
World Almanac® Library editorial direction: Mark J. Sachner
World Almanac® Library art direction: Tammy West
World Almanac® Library production: Jessica Morris
World Almanac® Library editors: Monica Rausch, Carol Ryback

Photo credits: Courtesy Central Pacific Railroad Photographic History Museum © 2004, CPRR.org: 10;
Denver Public Library Western History Collection: 19, 21, 29, 39, 40, 42, 43; Library of Congress: cover,
4, 5, 7, 13, 15, 16, 17, 18, 23, 28, 30, 34, 36, 37; National Archives: 8, 27, 32, 35, 41; NDSU Archives/
Fred Hulstrand Collection: 22, 24, 38, 44; Union Pacific Railroad Museum: 11.

Printed in Canada

1 2 3 4 5 6 7 8 9 09 08 07 06 05

Contents

Chapter 1: The Homestead Act   4

Chapter 2: Railroads and Land Wars   10

Chapter 3: The Trip West   16

Chapter 4: Establishing a Claim   22

Chapter 5: Farming the Homestead   28

Chapter 6: The Life of a Homesteader   34

Chapter 7: Earning Title to Land   40

Conclusion   44

Time Line   45

Glossary   46

Further Information   47

Index   48

The Homestead Act

The United States began as a small country with just thirteen states located along the East Coast of North America. Not content with its small size, the United States quickly entered a period of westward expansion, which lasted from 1803 until about 1912.

Manifest Destiny—the belief that Americans' God-given right was to assume control of the continent, spreading U.S. ideas and government to new peoples and territories along the way—shaped U.S. land policy during this era. The U.S. government purchased land from other countries or conquered territory by taking land from Native peoples until the United States stretched from coast to coast.

◀ In 1830, President Andrew Jackson began the policy of removing Native Americans from their homelands to make room for U.S. settlers.

Native American Removal

As the United States expanded its western boundaries, the lives of Native Americans changed forever. For thousands of years, Native American groups lived on the land, but many politicians saw these American Indian civilizations as obstacles to settlement by Anglos, or people of non-Spanish, European descent.

President Andrew Jackson (1829–1837) asked, "What good man would prefer a country covered with forest and ranged by a few thousand savages to our extensive republic, studded with cities, towns, and prosperous farms and filled with all the blessings of liberty, civilization and religion?" Beginning in 1830, President Jackson enforced a Native American removal policy. He took Native American land and ordered U.S. troops to forcibly relocate Indians to reservations to make room for more Anglo settlers. By the 1860s, the U.S. government had millions of open acres (hectares) of land in the public domain. Public-domain land is land that is owned and controlled by the government.

Most of this public land was in the western interior of the United States in what are now Kansas, Oklahoma, Nebraska,

▲ Apache Chief Geronimo (bending over buffalo) on his last buffalo hunt in Oklahoma in 1906. Native Americans used almost every part of the buffalo they killed—the hide for making clothes and shoes, the bones for tools, and even the bladder as a pouch or medicine bag.

the Dakotas, and Montana. This area's arid climate, with its few rivers and mostly flat and treeless terrain, had earned it the nickname "great American desert." Early settlers in the 1840s had described the area as a "sea of grass" and bypassed it to settle in California and the more humid Pacific Northwest. By the early 1860s, the East and West Coasts were home to centers of large population, but the interior of the country was largely unpopulated after the removal of the Native American groups.

The Politics of Land Grants

By the mid-1800s, the issue of slavery began to divide the United States. Thousands of African American slaves worked in the plantations and mines of the South. Southern states believed that slavery should continue to be legal, while many Northern states felt it should be outlawed.

The slavery debate influenced the land-grant policy that governed western territory. Northern states were more populous than Southern states, and the majority of the settlers moving West were antislavery Northerners. Some Northern leaders even formed the Free-Soil Party to encourage western settlement and the formation of antislavery territories. The South worried that this western settlement would shift the balance of federal power toward free states as the western territories, comprised mainly of former Northerners, created antislavery states and gained votes in Congress. To stop this, Southern congressmen consistently voted down any proposals in Congress that called for improvement to the West, such as the building of roads, railroads, or canals to speed transportation to remote areas, that might make settlement more appealing to Northerners living in crowded cities.

Southern congressmen also opposed liberal land laws that offered inexpensive or free land because the sale of public land

◀ This 1848 editorial cartoon mocks the alliance between the Free-Soil Democrats, Whig Party, and Liberty Party that resulted in the formation of the Free-Soil Party and the nomination of Free-Soil candidate Martin Van Buren for president.

raised money for the federal government. If land was given away free, they worried that money for the government would have to be raised in another way, such as charging tariffs, or taxes, for trade. The Southern economy was based on free trade. They fought any policy that might result in tariffs on their agricultural exports because paying tariffs would reduce the profits from the sale of their goods.

Because Congress could not agree on a more liberal land policy, from 1820 to 1862, the Land Law of 1820 continued to govern settlers who wanted to move West. The 1820 law offered public lands for sale in 80-acre (32-ha) lots at $1.25 an acre. If a person could pay $100, he or she could buy land from the government. Unfortunately, many people could not afford $100, and the government did not offer smaller lots for sale. Land speculators bought up many lots and sold smaller amounts of acreage to people at higher prices, making enormous profit.

The Pre-emption Act of 1841

Throughout the 1820s to 1840s, thousands of settlers who could not afford to buy 80 acres (32 ha) at one time ignored the

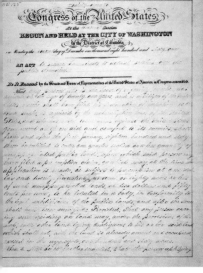

1820 land law and moved onto public domain land anyway. These people, known as squatters, built houses and farmed the land without receiving any legal title to it. Since they had no title to it, squatters often had their land sold by the government to legal settlers or land speculators, thus losing the benefits of the hard work they put into improving their land.

By 1840, however, there were so many of these illegal squatters, both Northern and Southern, that they pressured Congress into passing more liberal land laws. In 1841, Northern and Southern Congressional representatives voted together to pass the Pre-Emption Act of 1841, which allowed squatters to purchase the legal title to the land they occupied at the minimum price.

The Homestead Act

The Pre-Emption Act of 1841 helped squatters, but many people wanted even more from the government—they wanted free land. Congress debated several free land-grant acts in the 1850s, but Southern opponents refused to pass the acts.

With the start of the Civil War (1861–1865), however, the Southern states left the Union, and the Northern-controlled Congress was free to reshape U.S. western land policy. In 1862, Congress authorized funding for a Transcontinental Railroad to link all sections of the country.

The U.S. government wanted loyal Union settlers to occupy former Native American lands and establish towns loyal to U.S. interests. To encourage new settlement in the West, on May 20, 1862, Congress passed the Homestead Act, which opened 270 million acres (109 million ha), or 10 percent of the area of the United States, to settlement. Under this act, a person could "select any surveyed land up to 160 acres (65 ha) and . . . gain title to it after five years' residence, making prescribed improvements, and paying a modest fee for the service of the register and the receiver." The required improvements were building a home, living on the homestead, and farming and fencing a certain portion of the land.

Any heads of households, including women and free African Americans, who were twenty-one years old or older and a citizen, or intending to become a citizen, of the United States, could claim land under the Homestead Act. Union soldiers or their widows could deduct time served in the army from the five-year residence requirement. Convinced of Manifest Destiny, thousands of people journeyed to the western interior in search of free land and the wealth they hoped it would bring.

Daniel Freeman (1826-1908)

Daniel Freeman, a Union scout from Illinois stationed at Fort Leavenworth in Kansas, was the first person to file a homestead claim. He heard about the Homestead Act and took leave from military service to go to Nebraska and pick a claim about 50 miles (80 km) from what is now Lincoln. Freeman had to report for duty back in Kansas on January 1, 1863, the same day the Homestead Act became law. Freeman convinced a clerk to open the land office ten minutes after midnight so he could file a claim and still have time to travel back to Kansas to report for duty.

After the war, Freeman married Agnes Suiter from Iowa. Together, they built a farm and had eight children. Several of their children settled on the homestead, too. Today, Freeman's claim is the site of the Homestead National Monument of America.

Chapter 2

Railroads and Land Wars

In 1862, the same year the U.S. government enacted the Homestead Act, it also approved using federal money to fund a Transcontinental Railroad. Congress gave millions of acres (ha) of free land grants to railroad companies. As a reward for building track, railroad companies received right-of-way land grants that adjoined the track. These grants alternated in sections from one side of the track to the other. The alternating sections of land were quite valuable because future towns would be built there. Railroads then sold the choice land to settlers to finance building the tracks.

Homesteaders fought against the federal land grants to railroads because Congress often designated the best lands to the railroads. As a result, individual landowners often wound up

◀ These Central Pacific railroad workers are transporting wood to make into tracks in the mid-1800s. On average, work crews were laying 2 miles (3.2 km) of track each day to build the Transcontinental Railroad.

with inferior tracts and were forced to buy the better areas from the railroad companies. In this way, the U.S. government managed to get the homesteaders to finance part of the railroad companies' construction costs.

Even though homesteaders fought against land grants for railroads, they realized that trains were vital to their economic security. Railroads brought passengers, mail, and supplies to remote towns and provided a reasonably priced and fast way to transport goods to faraway markets.

The railroad also hastened westward settlement. Thousands of workers—mainly African Americans and Chinese and European immigrants—worked to clear the land and build the tracks. Towns formed along railroad stops, and the trains quickly brought hundreds of new settlers West. One railroad owner bragged that the railroad "civilized" the "wild" western territory and that he "conquered the West without firing a shot."

▼ This 1870s Union Pacific advertisement entices settlers to buy railroad land.

Railroad Boosters

The railroads had to sell millions of acres of land grants to make any profits. They faced the difficult task of selling their land when people could claim land for free under the Homestead Act. To do this, railroads formed land departments and immigration bureaus with boosters, now known as public relations (PR) people who handle promotions and marketing, in charge of luring European immigrants to settle on the railroads' land in the United States.

The railroads printed thousands of brochures and spent millions of dollars in advertising—much of it false or greatly

Railroads and the Decline of Buffalo

Scientists believe that about 60 million American bison, also known as buffalo, once roamed the Great Plains. By 1900, however, buffalo were almost extinct, and one cause was the expansion of the railroad.

To feed work crews, railroad companies hired professional buffalo hunters to obtain meat. They also organized moving buffalo hunts. Hunters could ride in train cars and shoot buffalo from open windows or doors. These hunts left hundreds of carcasses rotting next to the railroad tracks. After many passengers complained about the smell of the rotting meat, the railroad discontinued the trips.

The arrival of the railroad, hunters, and settlers greatly reduced wild game and buffalo in Native American hunting grounds. Many Plains Indian groups were nomadic people who traveled with the buffalo herds, relying on the animal for food. Some American Indian groups tried to protect their way of life by attacking settlers and the railroad crews.

The U.S. government encouraged the overhunting of buffalo. It built forts in the Plains area and sent soldiers to control Indian uprisings.

exaggerated. One railroad ad claimed the Great Plains land was so fertile that "you only have to tickle it with a plow and it will laugh a harvest that will gladden your hearts." Others incorrectly described the weather as a "temperate, invigorating, and mild climate, similar to that of Virginia" and reassured those who worried about the dryness of the area that "scientific" evidence showed that steam from the trains increased rain-cloud formation. Settlers soon found that their expectations of land in the Great Plains, based on the false railroad advertising, was far short of reality.

Railroads also offered inexpensive transportation to settlers willing to buy land. They often even deducted the cost of the ticket from the land fee. Once people settled on railroad land, the railroad company then funded improvement projects to encourage them to stay permanently. Railroad owners knew that successful settlers would need more freight services, which the railroad would offer—at a price.

Bonanza Farming

The Northern Pacific Railway created "bonanza farming." A bonanza farm was a farm consisting of at least one thousand or more acres (ha) of railroad land that used the latest technology to grow wheat crops. This railroad used bonanza farms to convince people of the quality of their land that was for sale.

The first bonanza farm on the Great Plains opened in 1874 when the railroad hired Oliver Dalrymple, an experienced farmer from Minnesota, to create a bonanza wheat farm in the Red River Valley of the Dakotas. Dalrymple relocated to railroad land in the Dakotas and started a wheat farm. He bought the best current farm equipment and hired farmhands. The equipment reduced labor and production costs, resulting in greater profits.

Railroads wrote ads and stories about Dalrymple's success and organized trips to his farm to show settlers what was possible. By 1877, many people had bought land from the railroad on which they started hundreds of new wheat farms in the Red River Valley.

Land Fraud

Railroads and land speculators frequently abused the Homestead Act by participating in land fraud, which is using trickery to

▲ Previous to bonanza farming, the Great Plains were known as the Great American Desert because of their dry soil and lack of trees. Bonanza farms in the Red River Valley, such as this 1914 experimental one in Williston, North Dakota, changed that impression.

obtain land illegally. Drifters were hired to pose as farmers and file a claim at the land office. The railroad and speculators then assumed control of the claims and sold them at a profit. To prevent land fraud, one of the requirements to obtain title was that the claimant live on the land and build a house. Some railroads and land speculator companies built small shacks on wheels and wheeled them from claim to claim when land inspectors were due to arrive.

A few individuals abused the Homestead Act, too. To increase their land holdings, farmers would often have their children—who were not yet twenty-one—file homestead claims. The system of recording births in the 1800s was not as formalized as it is today, so many land agents accepted the claimants' lies.

Land Wars

Throughout the 1800s, conflicts over land ownership frequently erupted in the West. Sometimes two settlers claimed the same homestead, and other times people argued over the boundaries of their land. Lawyers conducted a booming business representing claim disputes in court. Some land wars were not fought in court but broke out instead in bloody violence. Some of the deadliest fighting took place between ranchers and homesteaders.

Until the mid-1880s, most ranchers practiced an open-range style of livestock raising. Cattle wandered in public-domain lands, eating grass and drinking water where they found it. Twice each year cowboys rounded up the cattle and branded new calves. They then separated cattle to be sold and drove them thousands of miles (kilometers) to railroad depots in cow towns.

Homesteaders, however, believed in private ownership of land and often claimed public-domain land with prime grass and water for their homestead. They marked the borders of their land by planting hedges and were furious when open-range cattle wandered onto their land and trampled their crops. They frequently shot cattle that trespassed on their land, jokingly calling them "slow elk." Homesteaders believed that their grass should be reserved for their own livestock to eat, rather than another ranchers' cattle.

Until the 1870s, fences were rare on homesteads because the materials, such as wood or wire, were too expensive. In 1873, Jacob Glidden invented barbed wire, an inexpensive wire fence with jagged spikes on it. Soon, homesteaders were fencing their land with barbed wire. Cattle could no longer wander freely and find food, which put the open-range ranching system in danger.

Ranchers disliked homesteaders because of their private and possessive use of the land and referred to them as "nesters." During the fence-cutter wars of the early 1880s, groups of cowboys put on hoods and sneaked around at night cutting hundreds of miles (km) of barbed-wire fencing. Homesteaders responded by posting armed guards who shot trespassers on sight. Cowboys fought back by killing homesteaders.

To settle the dispute between open-range ranchers and homesteaders, state leaders passed laws giving people the right to mark their territories with fences and making it illegal to cut fences. Even though they also outlawed the policy of fencing land without owning the title to it, the homesteaders had won the battle, and open-range ranching was nonexistent by 1890.

▲ One of the myth-like figures of the West, cowboys actually had a hot, dusty, smelly, and difficult job. Here, they brand cattle in the late 1800s with a red-hot branding iron on the open range, before fencing ended the need for this type of ranching.

Chapter 3

The Trip West

By the end of the Civil War in 1865, only about 15,000 people had filed Homestead claims, but after the war, thousands of people moved West to make a claim. A popular song of the time expressed the optimism of these settlers: "Come along, come along, don't be alarmed; Uncle Sam is rich enough to give us all a farm!"

People moved West for many different reasons. Some were veterans of the Civil War who could claim title to land without waiting five years, and others were women or former slaves who dreamed of owning their own property. Some farmers moved West in search of more fertile land, while immigrants from Europe left their countries to escape poverty or poor living conditions and start fresh in the United States.

Most homesteaders moved West in large family groups and usually settled on adjoining homesteads. Home-steading immigrants wrote letters to

◀ Homesteaders like these in 1862 packed their wagons as full as possible with supplies before heading West.

family and friends in their home countries, describing good locations for settlement and encouraging them to come and claim free land. If new immigrants came, they often settled near their friends or relatives who had already filed a claim. Soon, large communities of diverse ethnic groups dotted the Great Plains.

Preparing for the Trip

The trip West was expensive, and homesteaders often saved for years and sold most of their possessions to buy the transportation and supplies they would need for their new life.

Those people that traveled by steamboat on the Mississippi or Missouri Rivers from the eastern United States had to purchase tickets for about $300 and pay shipping costs of 12 cents per pound (26 cents per kilogram) for their supplies. Railroads often advertised special rates for homesteaders, but the trip was still expensive and uncomfortable, with thirty or more people crowded into one railroad car. They had no privacy or separate sleeping areas and were forced to share one common toilet and cookstove.

▼ Some settlers took steamboats to St. Louis, a main departure point for wagon trains heading West. This illustration depicts steamboats racing from New Orleans to St. Louis in 1870.

The most popular transportation for homesteaders were covered wagons pulled by oxen, which together cost about $400. The typical wagon was about 14 feet (4 meters) long, 4 feet (1.2 m) wide, and 2 feet (.6 m) deep and made of a strong wood, such as hickory, maple, or oak. Storage compartments inside the wagon held a family's possessions. For

▶ Oxen pull covered wagons in a wagon train in the Black Hills of South Dakota in 1887. The wagons were nicknamed "prairie schooners" for their resemblance to boats floating on the "sea of grass" that was the Great Plains.

protection from bad weather, the wagon box was covered with a thick cotton cover nicknamed a "bonnet." U-shaped wooden supports held the bonnet in place over the wagon box, with openings in the front and back to let in fresh air. To waterproof the outfit, settlers rubbed linseed oil or tallow (hard animal fat) on the bonnet and nailed animal hides to the outside of the wagon box.

Most homesteaders needed to have at least $1,000 worth of supplies to successfully last the first winter on their new claim. Towns were few and far between, and homesteaders needed to be self-sufficient to survive. They needed farming equipment, seeds, tools, food, clothes, livestock, eating utensils, a stove, replacement wagon parts, water barrels, guns, and ammunition. One wagon could carry up to 2,500 pounds (1,134 kg) of supplies, but unneeded items, such as books or furniture, were often abandoned along the side of the trail if the oxen grew too tired to pull the heavy load.

The Journey

There were few roads in the far West, and most that existed were poorly maintained. After leaving eastern areas with farms and good roads, most early homesteaders had to blaze at least one section of their own trail. The trip was dusty and very bumpy, and wagons often got stuck in mud or sand. Most wagons were so heavily loaded with supplies that they only traveled about 2 miles (3 km) per hour. One writer in the St. Joseph, Missouri, *Gazette*, described the homesteaders' journey in this way, "A man must be able to endure heat like a Salamander, mud and water like a muskrat, dust like a toad, and labor like a jackass. He must learn to eat with his unwashed fingers, drink out of the same vessel as his mules, sleep on the ground when it rains, and share his blanket with vermin, and have patience with musketoes . . . It is hardship without glory."

◀ This family is traveling through Loup Valley, Nebraska, in search of a homestead in 1886.

Native Americans and Homesteaders

To make room for more Anglo settlers in the East, beginning in the 1820s, the U.S. Army gathered thousands of Native Americans there and forced them into Indian Territory (what is now Oklahoma), a large section of western land set aside for Native groups in a series of government treaties. These treaties made it illegal for Anglos to use or settle on that land without permission, so people often paid tolls to the local tribes to herd cattle or pass through Indian land. Despite these treaty agreements, some Anglos used the land illegally, and many Natives resisted the presence of non-Natives in Indian Territory.

By the late 1870s, some Anglos, known as boomers, wanted to take back the land in Indian Territory and open it to non-Indian settlement. In 1879, boomers from Kansas and Missouri illegally settled in Indian Territory, but the U.S. Army forced them to leave. More Anglo American settlers followed, and they were all evicted, fined $1,000, or arrested by U.S. troops. Despite Native American protests, the U.S. government eventually granted Anglo demands. In 1889, land in the Indian Territory was opened for settlement by non-Natives.

The wagon trip West was also dangerous, because settlers could be attacked by bandits or by Native groups unhappy with the presence of Anglos on their land. Usually, a few families from the same town traveled together in a wagon train made of several wagons for more safety. The settlers circled the wagons at night and kept watch for attackers. The group also worked together to fix broken wagons and to move their wagons across streams or rivers.

Despite the added protection offered by groups who traveled together, many people died on the journey—most from accidental gunshot injuries, drowning while crossing rivers, or illness, such as smallpox, scurvy, or typhoid. Also, the heavy wagons were difficult to stop once started, and the oxen or wagon wheels injured some pioneers. Children sometimes fell out of the wagon and were run over by the wheels, and women's skirts could be caught in the wheels, pulling them under the wagon. If they were not watched closely, children

could wander too far from the slow-moving wagons and get lost or be attacked and killed by animals.

Picking a Claim

The homesteaders who survived the trip to their desired destination began looking for the best land to claim. The most desirable homesteads were those that included or were near water or railroad lines. These choice claims were quickly snatched, and other homesteaders were forced to choose claims farther away.

After choosing land, the first thing a homesteader did was mark his or her claim so that others would know that it was taken. To do this, they might dig a ditch or put ropes or stakes around their homestead's borders. They then went to the land office and began the process of legally filing a claim.

▲ Men use a rope to stake a homestead claim near Craig, Colorado, about 1913. Settlers with desirable claims had to be careful to stake their claims well, or the stakes could be moved, stolen, or knocked over by other homesteaders or speculators trying to move in on their land.

Establishing a Claim

Once homesteaders staked their claims, they visited the nearest local land office to officially register their intentions. At the land office, the U.S. government land agent checked the survey and recorded the specific boundaries of the homestead. They checked to make sure the land was unclaimed and in the public domain. If the land was not yet claimed, the homesteader paid a registration fee of $10, which established a temporary claim on the land. The land agent received a $2 fee.

The process of performing the required government land improvements was called "proving up." After gaining temporary claim to the land at the land office, homesteaders returned to their claim to begin the process of improving the land in order to gain a permanent title after the five-year residency requirement.

◀ One sign of "proving up" was a glass window in a homesteader's house. These children are pictured outside the Malken family sod house in 1895 in North Dakota.

Building a House

One of the first improvements a homesteader made to his or her claim was building a house. Provisions to the Homestead Act required that to obtain legal title to land, the house built there must contain at least one glass window and be at least 10 by 12 feet (3 by 3.7 m) in size. Most homesteaders had spent the majority of their money outfitting themselves with supplies for the trip and first winter and could not afford expensive materials to build their homes, so they creatively built homes from whatever natural materials they could find.

The type of materials available for construction depended on the location of the homestead. In rocky areas, homesteaders quarried stone to use for building. Clay could be formed into bricks and hardened to build shelters. In forested areas where timber was available, log cabins—introduced by Swedish immigrants in the 1700s—were the most popular housing choice and could be built in two to three days.

To build a log cabin, homesteaders first built a raised stone foundation to keep the logs from touching the wet ground, thus reducing the likelihood that the wood would rot. Next, they cut down trees and removed the branches to create long logs. Then, they cut a notch in each end of the logs and fit the logs together, at 90-degree angles, to create corners. They stacked

▲ Homesteading couple outside their log cabin on their claim in Alaska around 1900. Log cabins were a popular choice for homes near a source of timber because they could be built easily and with few tools—just an axe and an auger, which is a hole-boring tool.

the notched logs to form the walls and then built a slanted roof out of wooden planks. To seal the cracks between the logs, settlers stuffed wood chips and branches into the gaps. They then mixed sand, dirt, and water to make a cement-like paste, which they spread over the cracks.

Timber, however, was scarce on the Great Plains. The flat land was covered as far as the eye could see by tall grasses broken only by a few scattered pockets of cottonwood trees that grew along streams or creeks. A Great Plains homesteaders' first house was often their wagon or a dugout that they carved out of a hillside. If there was no hill on the claim, a homesteader might dig a hole in the ground and cover it with a wagon wheel to serve as temporary shelter. For a more permanent house, homesteaders were forced to invent a new type of building by using the material beneath their feet—sod. In fact, sod was such an important building material on the prairies that it was nicknamed "Nebraska marble," and homesteaders were called "sodbusters."

The roots of certain types of prairie grass, such as wheat grass or buffalo grass, grew so tightly together that they held dirt together like bricks when cut. Homesteaders sliced slabs out of the hard sod and stacked the slabs grass-side down to build sod houses with thick walls. Often, a branch or cottonwood-frame roof topped the house. This, too, pioneers covered with slabs of sod but facing up this time. Mark Twain found these grass roofs interesting, writing that "it was the first time we had ever seen a man's front yard on top of his house."

▼ This family wears its Sunday best in the early 1900s for a photo by a traveling photographer. Their sod home would have been referred to as a "soddy" or a "dobie."

No Renters Here

In 1873, homesteader Uriah Oblinger wrote letters back home describing life in Nebraska.

" Most all of the people here live in Sod houses and dug outs. I like the sod house the best—they are the most convenient. I expect you think we live miserable because we are in a sod house. But I tell you in solid earnest, I never enjoyed myself better. But George, I expect you are ready to say, It is because it is something new. No, this not the case. It is because we are on our own, and the thoughts of moving next spring does not bother me. Every lick we strike is for ourselves and not half for some one else. I tell you this is quite a consolation to us who have been renters so long. There are no renters here. Everyone is on his own and doing the best he can. "

Homesteaders let the walls settle for several weeks, then usually coated the inside with plaster or whitewash paste. The floor was dirt or gravel and was raked several times a day to keep it even.

Sod houses had advantages—they were cheap and lasted about seven years. The dirt held between the prairie-grass roots was a good insulator, making houses cool in summer and warm in winter. The homes withstood fire and wind well, but insects, snakes, and mice lived in the dirt walls and frequently tunneled into the interior of the house.

Sod houses were also quite messy. During windstorms, a steady stream of dirt trickled from the roof and walls into the house. If they had the material available, women tacked sheets or cloth over the ceiling to stop the falling dirt. Nothing, however, could keep out the rain. Rainwater mixed with the dirt, causing mud to drip into the house, and too much rain would weaken the roof enough to make it collapse.

If homesteaders were successful and earned enough profit from their crops, they imported timber to build more permanent wood-framed homes. They tacked tar paper, old newspapers, or pages torn from catalogs on the walls to help

On April 22, 1889, the first land rush in U.S. history occurred when people from around the world came to settle the newly opened land in Indian Territory. At noon on April 22, military officers signaled the opening of the land. Instantly, about fifty thousand people on wagons, trains, or horses dashed into the territory in a wild race to claim one of the twelve thousand available homesteads in what is now Oklahoma.

Towns were created in just one day. A reporter from the Kansas *Nationalist* wrote that in the 1889 land rush "the people went out like flies out of a sugar cask, and in five minutes a square mile [2.6 sq km] of the prairie was spotted with squatters looking like flies on a sticky paper . . . we passed populous towns, built in an hour . . . we had seen the sight of the century."

The U.S. government continued to buy or take away land from Native American nations, and homesteaders claimed more former Indian land during the land rushes of 1891, 1893, 1901, and 1911. The largest rush took place in 1893, when about one hundred thousand people raced to claim homesteads in Oklahoma.

stop wind from seeping through any cracks in the wood.

Water and Fuel

Finding water to drink was just as important as building a house. Those homesteaders not lucky enough to be near water had to haul it in buckets or barrels from faraway creeks or rivers. If there was no water within traveling distance, homesteaders caught rainwater in cisterns or rain barrels. In winter, they melted snow for water.

To create a permanent water supply, homesteaders dug wells. If they were near a water source, the well did not have to be deep because water was near the surface. In the arid plains, however, homesteaders had to tunnel 300 feet (91 m) or more to tap into groundwater. Digging a well this deep took a lot of time and effort. If settlers could afford it, they would hire a professional well digger. Like traveling salespeople, these men traveled from homestead to homestead to sell their services. In the 1880s,

homesteaders began digging wells with new equipment that had been invented for drilling oil.

Homesteaders used a bucket lowered with rope to get water from shallow wells, but deeper wells required power to move the water up from the ground. By the 1870s, homesteaders were using windmills to harness the prairie wind for energy to pump water to the surface. The windmills also powered gristmills, which ground grain.

All homesteaders had fireplaces or small stoves inside their houses, and they needed fuel to heat their homes and cook their food. Settlers in forested areas cut timber to burn. On the prairies, where little timber existed, sodbusters found other forms of fuel. They burned buffalo or cow chips, the dried waste material left behind by passing buffalo and cow herds. When dried manure was unavailable, settlers burned hay, grass, or mesquite roots.

▲ Texans use mules to haul water in barrels to their homestead in 1905. Homesteaders reused their precious water in many ways to avoid having to haul it from far away. Most bathed only once a week, and then the whole family used the same water. Afterwards, the water was used for laundry.

Chapter 5

Farming the Homestead

Cultivating at least 10 acres (4 ha) of a homestead's land was necessary both for earning a permanent title to land under the Homestead Act and for making a living. Not only did farmers have to grow enough food for their families, but they also had to have a surplus crop to sell for supplies and equipment. This task proved difficult for the majority of homesteaders.

Many homesteaders who moved West in search of free land had no previous farming experience. Farming in the dry climate of the Great Plains was a challenge to even the most experienced farmers, and many homesteaders abandoned their claims because they did not have the farming skills to survive. Only about 40 percent of homesteaders earned the final title to their claim.

◀ Farming was so crucial to a family's livelihood that children were often kept home from school to work on the farm. These children are missing school to plow a field in Kentucky in the early 1900s.

Farming Techniques

Preparing land for farming was hard work. Farmers in forested areas had to clear trees before planting crops. Great Plains farmers had to break up the sod before they could plant anything. All homesteaders faced the constant battle of preventing wild animals from eating their crops.

Homesteaders often had trouble finding enough water. Many dug wells, and some used windmills to pump water to the surface. Sometimes even that did not provide enough water to irrigate crops. Farmers near streams and rivers dug ditches to channel water into their fields.

Irrigation, however, was not always possible. Farmers in the Great Plains developed dry farming, which consisted of new land-management techniques to farm without much water. Farmers divided their fields into strips, leaving every other strip fallow—plowed but left unseeded—each year. They placed a layer of mulch over the ground to seal in the moisture. Farmers rotated which strips were left fallow every year so that whatever field they planted had two years' worth of moisture, one year of which was stored in the soil. Other techniques were also used, such as shallow cultivation that killed moisture-stealing weeds.

 Dry farming methods were used by farms in many areas, including this rye farm in Colorado in 1908. Besides leaving fields fallow, farmers on dry land also used wide plow sweeps, which left dead plant material covering the land. This material helped keep moisture from evaporating from the soil.

Farming Technology

New technology also was needed to make farming the Great Plains possible. The cast-iron plows that existed when the first

▶ An African American farmer plows a Virginia field in about 1899. Farmers plowed fields in order to destroy old vegetation and expose the richer soil underneath.

homesteaders moved to the Great Plains barely cut through the tough sod and dirt stuck to it and had to be scraped off by hand. To fill the need, Illinois native John Deere invented the steel plow in 1837. Thousands of homesteaders used Deere's heavy-machinery, and his company still exists today. In 1868, inventor and Scotsman James Oliver from Indiana invented an improved chilled-iron plow in 1868. A special manufacturing process using cold water cooled the iron quickly, making it harder than cast-iron plows. The farmer used horses, mules, or oxen to pull the plow, which created a deep furrow through the earth where seeds were then planted.

Other inventors created additional time- and labor-saving devices. The new breaker plow made wider furrows. Mechanical reapers made harvesting grain faster and automatic binders quickly gathered the grain and bound it into sheaves, which were bundles of plant stalks bound together with straw or twine.

New technology was both a blessing and a curse to homesteaders. Farmers needed the equipment to make the farm profitable, but they had to go heavily into debt to buy the expensive machines. They often sought loans from banks or mortgaged their land to obtain the necessary funds. If crops failed due to a natural disaster, farmers lost their farms to the bank.

An Insuperable Obstacle

Homesteaders were able to settle land once considered unfit for farming. The U.S. government hired Major Steven Long to conduct an exploration of the Great Plains region from 1819 to 1820. In his report, he concluded that the area was

" almost wholly unfit for cultivation, and of course uninhabitable by a people depending upon agriculture for their subsistence. Although tracts of fertile land considerably extensive are occasionally met with, yet the scarcity of wood and water, almost uniformly prevalent, will prove an insuperable obstacle in the way of settling the country. **"**

Crops

Farmers soon realized they would not only have to change their farming methods and technology, but they also had to plant different crops as well. Traditional eastern crops, such as corn, millet, sorghum, barley, and soft winter wheat, did not thrive in many areas of the Great Plains. Instead, farmers began experimenting with new grains brought by Europeans to the United States.

Homesteaders also discovered new varieties of wheat that were best suited to the farms of the Great Plains. Farmers in Kansas and Nebraska began growing hard-kerneled "Turkey Red" wheat from Crimea, while northern European spring wheat grew well in Montana, Minnesota, and the Dakotas.

▲ This sandstorm engulfed Midland, Texas, on February 20, 1894. It buried buildings and crops.

Old methods of using millstones to grind grain did not work with these hard-kerneled wheat varieties. To solve this problem, engineers invented chilled-iron rollers to mill grain, making it possible by the early 1880s to produce fine flour from the hard wheat.

Natural Disasters

Even with water and the current technology, however, farmers were not guaranteed a good harvest. Natural hazards on the Great Plains could destroy a whole season's crop in an instant.

Fire was a major danger on the dry grassy prairies and could be started at any time by a lightning strike or a spark from a campfire. Once started, the fire would quickly ignite more grass and speed across the plains, burning everything in its path. Many homesteaders tried to protect their homes by digging ditches, which served as firebreaks, a short distance

Life Is Too Short

In 1919, Mrs. H. C. Stuckey wrote about her experiences in a sod house in Nebraska.

" From hardly any rain we soon had more than we needed. Our roof would not stand the heavy downpours that sometimes contuned (sic) for days at a time, it would leak from one end to the other. We could keep our beds comparatively dry by drawing them into the middle of the room directly under the peak of the roof. Sometimes the water would drip on the stove while I was cooking, and I would have to keep tight lids on the skillets to prevent the mud from falling into the food. With my dress pinned up, and rubgers [sic] on my feet, I waded around until the clouds rolled by. Then we would clean house. Almost everything had to be moved outdoors to dry in the sun. Life is too short to be spent under a sod roof. "

from their houses. A firebreak might save a house during a fire, but the crops would be burned.

Even with improved dry-farming methods and irrigation, long periods of drought could make crops wither in the field. Windstorms, sandstorms, and tornados were other hazards to dry-farming methods. If strong winds blew the topsoil or mulch from fallow fields, the ground would lose the moisture that had been accumulating. Strong windstorms could create raging dust storms, which blew away fertile soil and sometimes even seeds.

Insect infestations were another hazard to homesteaders. In 1874, a devastating swarm of locusts infected the Great Plains from the Dakotas to Texas. The voracious insects ate almost everything—crops, shoes, and even wooden farm equipment handles. They piled knee deep in the fields, and railroads hired people to shovel them away from the tracks.

Chapter 6

The Life of a Homesteader

A homestead had to be mostly self-sufficient because the nearest towns were usually hundreds of miles away. Once or twice each year, a member of the family—usually the head of the household—would journey to town to buy supplies. If settlers ran out of something, they had to borrow from a neighbor or live without it.

Farming was hard work and a family effort, and most homesteaders, even children, worked from dawn until dusk performing chores, such as planting, harvesting, tending livestock, making soap or candles, doing laundry, sewing, cooking, or cleaning house.

Food

Finding and preparing a variety of food was important to the health of homesteaders. Diseases developed if homesteaders did not include fresh fruit

◀ Everyone in a homesteading family helped with chores. In this scene reminiscent of early homesteading, a Georgia woman chops wood to fuel her stove in 1941.

or vegetables in their diets for long periods of time. Lack of vitamin C from citrus fruits often caused scurvy, a dangerous disease with symptoms that included extreme weakness, bleeding gums, and bleeding under the skin. To keep a healthy diet, farmers grew fruits and vegetables in gardens and also picked wild fruits, such as raspberries and currants, during the summer.

Preserving these foods for eating year-round, however, was one of the biggest challenges a homesteader faced. Household refrigerators were not invented until the 1900s, so people dug underground root cellars to keep foods cool and dry. Some lucky towns near water sources had icehouses that were built below ground and lined with insulating materials, such as sawdust. During the winter, people chopped thick river or lake ice with axes and transported chunks to the icehouse. Throughout the summer, people could buy ice for iceboxes that kept food cold. Even iceboxes, however, could keep meat and fruits fresh only for a short time before they spoiled.

Farmers soon found other food-preservation techniques. They dried fruit and vegetables by leaving them to bake in the sun. Later, to eat the fruit, they soaked it in water until it was moist again. Sometimes they also canned fruit and made jams, jellies, soups, or sauces.

For meat, homesteaders usually hunted deer, rabbits, beaver, or whatever animals lived in their area. For

▼ To have a variety of food around, pioneer families often planted two gardens—one in the spring, which included greens and peas, and one later in the summer, which included heartier plants such as potatoes, squash, and beans. This Oklahoma family picks cherries to eat in 1900.

▲ This boy helps gather food for his family by hunting rabbits in 1908.

special occasions—or if wild game was unavailable—they slaughtered livestock, such as pigs, chickens, or cattle, to eat. They had to preserve this meat quickly because it could rot in an afternoon. Drying, smoking, and salting were the most common methods of meat preservation. For smoking, people butchered animals and hung pieces of the meat on hooks in small, specially built smokehouses. Homesteaders had to keep a fire smoking inside the smokehouse for weeks at a time or the meat would spoil. To salt meat, they sliced it thinly and placed the slices in a barrel on layers of salt and brine (water containing large amounts of salt). Before eating salted meat, homesteaders would have to thoroughly soak and scrub it to remove excess salt and make it edible.

Social Life

Despite being busy with hours of hard work farming and preserving food, some homesteaders felt isolated on their claims.

Since each homestead was 160 acres (64 ha), the closest neighbor lived at least .25 mile (.4 km) away. In more remote areas, homesteads might be hundreds of miles apart. People often did not see neighbors for weeks or months at a time. Some homesteaders were accustomed to busy cities and found the loneliness hard to bear. They looked forward to social occasions and celebrated together whenever possible.

▲ In a scene reminiscent of early homesteading families, this family is working together to sew a quilt in Gees Bend, Alabama, in 1937. Many of the quilts made in Gees Bend are now considered works of art.

Homesteading communities held large social events called "bees" for a variety of reasons but mainly to share a difficult workload. During quilting bees, women gathered together to help each other sew quilts. Each fall at the harvest bee, people worked together to harvest crops. To build barns or other buildings, a homesteader would host a building bee. Pioneers worked hard and played hard—most work-related bees concluded with an evening of food, dancing, and singing. As more homesteaders settled an area, they planned social bees that featured literature readings or spelling and singing contests.

Education

The first homesteaders taught their children at home with whatever books they had available. As more people moved into an area, the local homesteaders with children contributed to a school fund. They hired a teacher who was usually boarded in the farmers' homes and who moved from homestead to homestead during the school year.

Newly homesteaded areas had limited supplies, and early schools were often housed in barns or available outbuildings. As an area developed and prospered, however, settlers worked together to pay for and build a one-room schoolhouse. This building was often small and had one stove in the front to heat it. Maps and chalkboards were luxury items, and often schools in poor areas had no pencils, pens, or books. The schoolteacher was in charge of cleaning the building and procuring supplies, such as firewood for the stove.

In these schoolhouses, students of all ages and grades gathered together in one room to receive instruction. Younger children usually sat in the front, and older children sat in desks in the back of the room. All their desks faced the teacher's desk in the front of the room. Paper was expensive, so students wrote their lessons on small slates that—like chalkboards—could be erased and reused.

Students did not all have the same textbook, and teachers had to create lessons based on whatever books were available, which could prove

The Teaching Profession

Most towns preferred to hire male teachers but reluctantly turned to single women when no men were available. Women were paid less than men; they received about $54 per month while men received about $71. Female teachers often supplemented their low income by homesteading, too.

Rules governing teachers were strict in the 1800s. If a woman married, she was no longer allowed to teach school. This policy resulted in a high turnover rate, and by the late 1870s about one-quarter of the U.S. Anglo female population had taught school at some time.

A one-room schoolhouse in Fort Lupton, Colorado, in 1895. Scheduling of classes on the frontier depended on the needs of the farm. Children had to be home to help with chores, including planting and harvesting the crops.

challenging. Most lessons were fifteen minutes long and consisted of spelling, reading, writing, history, and arithmetic. Memorization was a popular teaching method of the time, and students often had to recite long passages in front of the class.

Teachers had almost complete authority over students and discipline was often harsh. If students misbehaved, teachers whipped them with a hickory switch (branch cut from a hickory tree) or whacked their hands with a ruler. Boys and girls were strictly separated. If caught playing together, they faced four lashes from the teacher. Swearing, playing cards, talking in class, forgetting lessons, or lying also resulted in a whipping.

Chapter 7

Earning Title to Land

At the end of five long years, a homesteader could finally obtain the legal title to his or her land. To do this, they had to prove that they had completed the provisions of the Homestead Act.

Proof of Claim

When homesteaders were ready to take legal possession of their land, they found two friends or neighbors who were willing to vouch for them. The witnesses had to have known them for two years and swear that the homesteader had actually improved, farmed, and lived on the claim. The witnesses filled out and signed a "proof form" that attested to the validity of the homesteader's claim. Sometimes a land agent would come and inspect the homestead to make sure it had been

◀ A homesteader's witness had to swear to the acreage and type of crops farmed on the claim. This man is plowing a field of peas on his homestead in Colorado in 1900.

improved, but other times the proof form would be accepted without a tour of the property.

Once the land agent accepted the proof, the homesteader paid a final $6 filing fee. The land agent then gave the homesteader the land patent, a legal document that transferred ownership from the government to the individual. Each land patent was signed with the name of the current president of the United States, and homesteaders used it to certify their ownership when they registered the land deed with the local government.

▲ Homesteaders filed their proof forms and registered their land claims at land offices like this one in Round Pound, Oklahoma, in 1894.

Evolution of the Homestead Act

The requirements to receive a land patent under the Homestead Act were challenging, and homesteaders eventually formed a group in 1867 called the Grange to lobby Congress for farmers' rights. One of their complaints was that the Homestead Act did not provide enough land in the dry Great Plains area to make a profit. Dryer land produced a lesser volume of crops, so more land was needed to create surplus crops to sell. To address this problem, Congress passed two additional provisions to the act.

The first provision was the Timber Culture Act of 1873, which granted an additional 160 acres (65 ha) of land to farmers if they agreed to plant 40 acres (16 ha) of trees. The government reduced the acreage of required timber planting to 10 acres (4 ha) in 1878.

▶ One way to irrigate land claimed under the Desert Land Act was to dig ditches through which water flowed. This method of irrigation was used to water the lettuce on this farm in 1943.

The second provision was the Desert Land Act of 1877, which affected arid regions of the west, including Arizona, California, the Dakotas, Idaho, Montana, Nevada, New Mexico, Oregon, Utah, Washington, and Wyoming. Under this provision, people could buy 640 acres (259 ha) of land for 25 cents per acre. In exchange, a homesteader had to irrigate the land within three years.

The General Public Lands Reform Act was passed in 1891. This act repealed the Timber Culture Act because of abuse by speculators. It also reduced land availible under the Desert Land Act to 320 acres (129.5 ha).

Legacy of the Homestead Act

By 1976, when the Homestead Act was officially repealed, about 1.6 million homestead applicants had improved the land and completed the five years necessary to receive land patents. A special provision for homesteading in Alaska existed until 1986.

The sodbusters forever changed the landscape of the West. New farming technology made it possible for homesteaders to quickly convert acres (ha) of wild grassland into farmland. The fences homesteaders built around land brought about the end of the open range and eventually closed the frontier.

As time passed, wood-frame houses and barns replaced sod houses, and large towns grew along railroad tracks. People built schoolhouses, churches, and stores to accommodate their growing population. Roads and railroad lines were built to reach newly homesteaded regions until the government declared the age of the frontier officially over in 1890.

A devastating result of homesteading the frontier was the destruction of the Native American lifestyle. Anglo home-steaders took Native American land and killed the buffalo the Indians relied on for survival.

▲ General stores, such as this one shown in 1890, sold supplies to homesteaders in areas that had been settled by enough families to support a store.

Homesteaders were convinced of their Manifest Destiny and harshly imposed U.S. government on Native groups. President Andrew Jackson justified his Indian removal policy by saying that it would "separate the Indians from immediate contact with settlements of whites . . . retard the progress of decay, which is lessening their numbers, and perhaps cause them gradually, under the protection of the government and through the influences of good counsels, to cast off their savage habits and become an interesting, civilized, and Christian community." For Native Americans, however, his removal policy and the later Homestead Act proved to create a legacy of death and destruction.

Today, the landscape of the western interior is changing into frontier again as the population decreases. Lack of industry in rural homesteaded areas has forced many younger people to leave in order to find jobs in large urban areas. It has also become increasingly difficult for small farms to be profitable, and the majority of small family farms are now owned by people aged fifty-five and older. Most farming in the Great Plains is now done by large corporations that use technology to farm large tracts of land with few workers. As a result, many areas of the Great Plains have only 6 people per square mile (sq km), which is the U.S. Census's definition of vacant land, or frontier.

Some people today feel the U.S. government should give back land on the Great Plains to Native American groups. They want to create a large prairie preserve where buffalo can roam once again.

No matter what the future of the Great Plains will be, the Homestead Act and the free land it offered came to symbolize— at least for those who were not being forced off their land—the American dream of a better life. Homesteaders journeyed over rugged land to face natural disasters and harsh climates, but many still managed to carve successful farms from the tough prairie land. The Homestead Act made westward settlement possible by giving free land to thousands of settlers who could not otherwise afford to purchase property.

▼ The U.S. Postal Service issued this stamp in 1962 to honor the Homestead Act's hundred-year anniversary. It pictures a homestead family outside their sod house in Nebraska.

1803: ▶ The United States doubles its size with land bought in the Louisiana Purchase.

1823: ▶ President James Monroe declares American intentions of expansion in a speech known as the Monroe Doctrine.

1830: ▶ Congress passes the Indian Removal Act, which legalized the removal and resettlement of Native American groups.

1837: ▶ Illinois native John Deere invents the steel plow.

1841: ▶ Congress passes the Pre-Emption Act, making it possible for squatters to purchase legal title to the land they had occupied at the minimum price.

1845: ▶ John O'Sullivan first uses term Manifest Destiny; Texas becomes a state.

1846: ▶ Mexican-American War begins.

1848: ▶ January 24—James Marshall finds gold at Sutter's Mill.
February 2—Mexican-American War ends when Treaty of Guadalupe Hidalgo is signed.

1850: ▶ California becomes a state.

1853: ▶ The United States buys more land from Mexico in the Gadsden Purchase.

1860: ▶ The Pony Express begins delivering mail.

1862: ▶ The Homestead Act—granting free land to settlers who farm and improve it for five years—becomes law.

1864: ▶ Nevada becomes a state.

1868: ▶ While living in Indiana, Scotsman James Oliver invents the chilled-iron plow.

1869: ▶ The Transcontinental Railroad is completed.

1873: ▶ Joseph Glidden invents barbed wire fencing; Congress passes the Timber Culture Act, which grants additional land to homesteaders who plant trees.

1874: ▶ Northern Pacific Railroad has Oliver Dalrymple open first bonanza wheat farm.

1877: ▶ Congress passes the Desert Land Act, making inexpensive public-domain land available to homesteaders who irrigate it.

1887: ▶ Congress passes the Dawes Act, which eliminates Native American traditional homelands.

1889: ▶ U.S. government opens land in the Indian Territory for non-Indian settlement.

1890: ▶ The U.S. government declares the frontier era is finished.

1898: ▶ United States annexes Hawaii.

1900: ▶ Hawaii becomes a U.S. territory.

1907: ▶ Oklahoma becomes a state.

1912: ▶ New Mexico and Arizona become states.

1934: ▶ Homestead Act is repealed.

1986: ▶ Homesteading ends in Alaska.

Anglo: person of non-Spanish, European descent

bee: a social gathering where people combine work, competition, and amusement

booster: an enthusiastic promoter

claim: something claimed in a formal or legal manner, especially a tract of public land staked out by a miner or homesteader

economy: system of producing and distributing goods and services

fallow: describing land plowed but left unseeded during a growing season

homestead: land claimed by a settler or squatter, especially under the Homestead Act

locust: any of numerous grasshoppers of the family Acrididae, which often migrate in immense swarms that can devour vegetation and crops

manifest: obviously true and easily recognizable. The term Manifest Destiny meant that the true and obvious destiny of the United States was to expand its borders to the Pacific Ocean.

millstone: one of a pair of cylindrical stones used in a mill for grinding grain

plow: a farm implement consisting of a heavy blade at the end of a beam, usually hitched to a draft team or motor vehicle and used for breaking up soil and cutting furrows in preparation for sowing

public domain: land owned and controlled by the state or federal government

range: an extensive area of open land on which livestock wander and graze

sod: a section of grass-covered surface soil held together by matted roots

squatter: a person who settles on unoccupied land without legal claim

tallow: animal fat used to make candles or soap

tariff: a list or system of duties, or taxes, imposed by a government on imported or exported goods

turnover: the number of workers hired by an establishment to replace those who have left in a given period of time

urban: of, relating to, or located in a city

whitewash: a mixture of lime and water, often with whiting, size, or glue added, that is used to whiten walls, fences, or other structures

whiting: a pure white grade of chalk that has been ground and washed for use in paints, ink, and putty